ALSO BY ROBERT PINSKY

POETRY

Sadness and Happiness

An Explanation of America

History of My Heart

The Want Bone

The Inferno of Dante: A New Verse Translation

The Figured Wheel: New and Collected Poems, 1966–1996

Jersey Rain

Gulf Music

Selected Poems

NONFICTION

*The Situation of Poetry: Contemporary
Poetry and Its Traditions*

Poetry and the World

The Sounds of Poetry: A Brief Guide

Democracy, Culture, and the Voice of Poetry

The Life of David

*Thousands of Broadways: Dreams and
Nightmares of the American Small Town*

*Singing School: Learning to Write (and
Read) Poetry by Studying the Masters*

AT THE FOUNDLING HOSPITAL

At the Foundling Hospital

Robert Pinsky

FARRAR STRAUS GIROUX / NEW YORK

Farrar, Straus and Giroux

18 West 18th Street, New York 10011

Copyright © 2016 by Robert Pinsky

Printed in the United States of America

First edition, 2016

Library of Congress Cataloging-in-Publication Data

Names: Pinsky, Robert.

Title: At the foundling hospital : poems / Robert Pinsky.

Description: First edition. | New York : Farrar, Straus and Giroux, 2016.

Identifiers: LCCN 2016007095 | ISBN 9780374158118 (hardcover) |
ISBN 9780374715472 (e-book)

Subjects: | BISAC: POETRY / American / General.

Classification: LCC PS3566.I54 A6 2016 | DDC 811/.54—dc23

LC record available at http://lccn.loc.gov/2016007095

Designed by Quemadura

Our books may be purchased in bulk for promotional, educational,
or business use. Please contact your local bookseller or the Macmillan
Corporate and Premium Sales Department at 1-800-221-7945,
extension 5442, or by e-mail at MacmillanSpecialMarkets@macmillan.com.

www.fsgbooks.com
www.twitter.com/fsgbooks
www.facebook.com/fsgbooks

1 3 5 7 9 10 8 6 4 2

To

LOUISE

And to the memory of
ALAN
and
CHARLIE

What is someone?

PINDAR

CONTENTS

AT THE FOUNDLING HOSPITAL

INSTRUMENT

It was a little newborn god
That made the first instrument:
Sweet vibration of
Mind, mind, mind
Enclosed in its orbit.

He scooped out a turtle's shell
And strung it with a rabbit's guts.
O what a stroke, to invent
Music from an empty case
Strung with bloody filaments—

The wiry rabbitflesh
Plucked or strummed,
Pulled taut across the gutted
Resonant hull of the turtle:
Music from a hollow shell
And the insides of a rabbit.
Sweet conception, sweet
Instrument of mind,

Mind, mind: Mind
Itself a capable vibration
Thrumming from here to there
In the cloven brainflesh
Contained in its helmet of bone—
Like an electronic boxful
Of channels and filaments
Bundled inside a case,
A little musical robot

Dreamed up by the mind
Embedded in the brain
With its blood-warm channels
And its humming network
Of neurons, engendering

The newborn baby god—
As clever and violent
As his own instrument
Of sweet, all-consuming
Imagination, held
By its own vibration:

Mind, mind, mind pulled
Taut in its bony shell,
Dreaming up Heaven and Hell.

PROCESSION

At the summit of Mauna Kea, an array of antennae
Sensitive to the colors of invisible light. Defiling

The sacred mountain, they tilt and sidle to measure
Submillimeter waves from across the universe:

System of cosmic removes and fine extremes
Devoted to track the wavering nature of things.

Your father Adam known also as Mākea,
Your mother Lakshmi known also as Eve:

Both of them smaller than the width of a hair,
They ride astride matched tortoises on a road

Nine microns wide, following another Eve
And another Adam all in a skybound procession

Of mothers and fathers, all the Lakshmis and Vishnus
Tendering you their Cain and you their Abel.

The snow Papa and the fire Pele observe tainting
Antennae controlled by a hand in Massachusetts.

Innumerable names and doings, innumerable
Destinies, remote histories, deities and tongues.

Somewhere among them your ancestor the slave,
Also your ancestors the thief the prince the stranger.

Each particle a thread of crazed pilgrim life
Passing as one tortoise mount pauses to tread

The emanation of a dead star still alive
And afire, back when the astral procession began.

Everybody by descent the outcome of a rape.
Everybody also the outcome of a great love.

Ruth, Holofernes, Sappho, Abelard, mostly
Anonymous traveling a filament of light

Across the nothing between the clouds of being
Into the pinhole iris of your mortal eye—

The heart of each telescope on Mauna Kea,
Is a tube finer than a hair on Vishnu's head.

On each hair of each Vishnu's head, a procession
Of subatomic tortoises crosses the universe.

In the skull of each tortoise in that procession
A faceted jewel attuned to a spectral channel

Where Kronos eats us his children, each contracting
By each one's nature a micron suture of light.

CREOLE

I'm tired of the gods, I'm pious about the ancestors: afloat in
The wake widening behind me in time, those restive devisers.

My father had one job from high school till he got fired at thirty.
The year was 1947 and his boss, planning to run for mayor,

Wanted to hire an Italian veteran, he explained, putting it
In plain English. I was seven years old, my sister was two.

The barbarian tribes in the woods were so savage the Empire
Had to conquer them to protect and clear its perimeter.

So into the woods Rome sent out missions of civilizing
Governors and forces to establish schools, courts, garrisons:

Soldiers, clerks, priests, citizens with their household slaves.
Years, decades, entire lives were spent in those hinterlands—

Which might be good places to retire on a government pension,
Especially if in your work-years you had acquired a native wife.

Often I get these things wrong or at best mixed up, but I do
Feel piety toward those persistent mixed families in Gaul,

Britain, Thrace. When I die may I take my place in the wedge
Widening and churning in the mortal ocean of years of souls.

The Roman colonizing and mixing, the Imperial processes
Of legal enslaving and freeing, involved not just the inevitable

Fucking in all senses of the word, but also marriages and births
As developers and barbers, scribes and thugs mingled and
    coupled

With the native people and peoples. Begetting and trading, they
Had to swap, blend and improvise languages—couples
    especially

Needed to invent French, Spanish, German: and I confess—
Roman, barbarian—I find that Creole work more glorious than
    God.

The way it happened, the school sent around a notice: anybody
Interested in becoming an *apprentice optician*, raise your hand.

It was the Great Depression, anything about a job sounded good to
Milford Pinsky, who told me he thought it meant a kind of dentistry.

Anyway, he was bored sitting in study hall, so he raised his hand,
And he got the job as was his destiny—full-time, once he graduated.

Joe Schiavone was the veteran who took the job, not a bad guy.
Dr. Vineburg did get elected mayor, Joe worked for him for years.

At the bank, John Smock, an Episcopalian whose family once owned
The bank, had played sports with Milford, and he gave him a small

Loan with no collateral, so he opened his own shop, grinding lenses
And selling glasses: as his mother-in-law said, "almost a Professional."

Optician comes from a Greek word that has to do with seeing.
Banker comes from an Italian word for a bench, where people
   sat,

To make loans or change. *Pinsky* like "Tex" or "Brooklyn" is
   a name
Nobody would have if they were still in that same place: those
   names all

Signify someone who's been away from home a while.
   Schiavone
Means "a Slav" or "slave." *Milford* is a variant on the poets'
   names—

Milton, Herbert, Sidney—certain immigrants used to give their
   offspring.
Creole comes from a word meaning to breed or to create, in a
   place.

MIXED CHORUS

My real name is Israel Beilin. My father
Was a Roman slave who gained his freedom.
I was first named Ralph Waldo Ellison but

I changed it to the name of one of your cities
Because I was born a Jew in Byelorussia.

I sit with Shakespeare and he winces not.

My other name is Flaccus. I wrote an essay
On the theme You Choose Your Ancestors.
It won't be any feeble, conventional wings

I'll rise on—not I, born of poor parents. Look:
My ankles are changed already, new white feathers

Are sprouting on my shoulders: these are my wings.

Across the color line I summon Aurelius
And Aristotle: threading through Philistine
And Amalekite they come, all graciously

And without condescension. I took the name
Irving or Caesar or Creole Jack. Some day they'll

Study me in Hungary, Newark and L.A., so

Spare me your needless tribute. Spare me the red
Hideousness of Georgia. I wrote your White
Christmas for you. And my third name, Burghardt,

Is Dutch: for all you know I am related to
Spinoza, Walcott, Pissarro—and in fact my

Grandfather Burghardt's first name was Othello.

NAMES

Arbitrary but also essential.

Before you can remember you will have found
You are Parvati or Adam, Anne or Laquan, all

With one same meaning: the meaning of the past,
A thunder cloud. Byron De La Beckwith, Primo Levi.
Medgar, Edgar, Hrothgar. Ishbaal.

Not just an allusion, but also an example:
Each with its meaning but also
An instance of the meaning of naming.

Lightning. Tamir. Abdi. Ikey Moe.
"What kind of name is that?"

Your own: the one word you can't ever
Hear clearly, but as in a carnival mirror.

Found and to find. Sandra Bland.
Tereke, Ehud. Jason. Duy. Quan.
Lost and to find,

Stammering Moses of Egypt, found
Afloat among bulrushes. Royal.

Aaron of Goshen, the articulate.

THE ORPHAN QUADRILLE

Lost arts of cochineal enamel and earthen bell foundry.
Shelling of the Parthenon, flooding of Sioux burials.
Let's caper in memory of our mothers and fathers.
   (*Step and turn, step to me darling*)

Faith-based razing of Buddhas, Torahs, Ikons
To obey Clerics, Committees, Scholars, Inquisitions.
Lost art of snake-handling, of speaking in tongues.
   (*Turn to me darling, skip to the trumpet*)

Lost arts of the poor, the Barrio Gótico overwhelmed
By galleries and bars. Let's rattle castanets to celebrate
A Thai restaurant and jazz club—we are not purists,
   (*Skip turn step, turn to the light*)

Our ancient glittering eyes grieve gaily. Lost arts of gay
Glitter, and of those school movies industries provided
When I was in the fifth grade: *The Story of Paper*,
   (*Children turn, turn where I tell you*)

Surprising Glass, Miracles of Petroleum. I worried our
Generation could never learn those industrial arts before
The adults died. "I *know* these kids—*we can't do it.*"
   (*Skip, slip and slide to me darling*)

But we did! Let's dance like the couple in clever fat-suits
Doing the Lindy Hop like it's nineteen-forty-seven. Jeté.
Dip. Double-time, stop-time. The Moonwalk, the Continental.
   (*Skip, skip, step to the light, turn to the side*)

THE FOUNDLING TOKENS

At the Foundling Hospital
For each abandoned
Baby a duly recorded token:
Bit of lace or a pewter brooch,
Identifying coin, button
Or bangle. One crushed thimble,
Noted at admission. Or paper:

At the Foundling Museum
A wall displaying hundreds
Of scraps, each pinned once
To some one particular infant's
Nightie, nappie or blanket,

Each with surviving particulate
Ink or graphite in studied lines
Betokening a life. Sometimes
A name—by rule never
To be used again for that
Foundling. And often,
Verses quoted or composed:

Hard is my Lot in deep Distress
To have no help where Most should find.
Sure Nature meant her sacred Laws
Should men as strong as Women bind.
Regardless he, Unable I,
To keep this image of my Heart
'Tis vile to Murder! hard to Starve
And Death almost to me to part!
If Fortune should her favours give
That I in Better plight may Live
I'd try to have my Boy again
And train him up the best of Men.

"To have" meaning to
Reclaim but also in the mind
To have again that same
Foundling, paternity
Regardless. The same
Boy again, reconceived.

Token meaning a least
Irreducible particle
Of meaning. Or *token* meaning
Token black, token woman,
Token gesture.

They sent the infant foundlings
To wet nurses, most of them
Out in the country. The foster
Mother by contract after
A few years returned the child
Ready for schooling
To the Foundling Hospital—

Unconsulted but retained
Relic syllables of a name
Or lines, bauble or needlework.

On the slave passage some Africans
Inscribed their true names into the hull
As though someday to be
Pronounced again.

Also the Chinese immigrants
In the dark Angel Island
Internment cells of San Francisco,
Many to be deported, wrote verses
Found on the walls above their bunks.

Fragment of a tune or a rhyme or name
Mumbled from memory. Incised
Into a bar of soap or even scraped

Into the very death-compound dirt
Or hut dirt or chalked onto pavement—
Scratched or smeared or intoned
Betokening. Or in the ordinary plight

Of insomnia reciting memorized
Avenues through the expanses
Of loss. Although almost never was
A foundling reclaimed, ever.

CULTURE

Bewildered, bewildering ape. Absinthe. Circumcision. Couplets.
Grudges, beliefs. War of my childhood, Europe tearing at itself.

Scarification. Conceptual art. Celebrated scholarly papers
On Trobriand Islanders, more fiction or poetry than science.

Absorbed deepest always invisibly now invisibly from a Cloud.
Visible and invisible in the old-style funny papers. The comics.

Images, meanings. In the old strip, the snob Maggie's hair
Climbed curly like the treble clef that embraces the musical G.

Her pugnosed husband Jiggs, a stocky bass clef, hair in two red
Tufts near his ears over the wing collar Maggie made him wear

Jiggs sneaking out a window for "corned beef and cabbage" at
"Dinty's"—how could a child guess it was code for Irish, beer?

In Africa I drank palm wine ladled from a red vinyl bucket.
The Sangoma who spoke with Ancestors was also a Christian.

A song: "I was drinking beer in a cabaret, Oh was I having fun!
Pistol-Packin' Mama caught me there—now I'm on the run."

The Web says it was a hit by Al Dexter the year I was born.
Mystified I absorbed it. "Obsessed" Allen Ginsberg read *Time*.

Cloudy explanations of Hutu and Tutsi: are they peoples or races
Or tribes or constructions out of the thin air of Rwandan history?

Music of stereotypes: pugnosed Irish Jiggs, "nouveau riche,"
Hillbilly in a cabaret, their forbidding Mamas objects of fear.

Charlie Chan. Life with Luigi. The Goldbergs. The Japanese
Sleuth Mr. Moto played by a Jew, Peter Lorre, who fled the Nazis.

Der Stürmer, lynchings, enclosures. T. S. Eliot's vicious lectures
On Culture, delivered in Virginia, a book he chose to suppress.

Virginia, Florida. Dakotas. In "California," word of no sure origin.
A young singer imitates the telltale *click* of Auto-Tune software

With her natural voice. Pearl Harbor: a Japanese movie sidekick
Became Filipino. Internment Camps. Quotas. Near Beer. Beauty.

Maggie and Jiggs had a beautiful daughter, Nora. The strip drawn
Beautifully by George McManus, inspired by Aubrey Beardsley.

Here he is posing in costume as Jiggs: as if it's all self-portrait—
Oh lay that pistol down, Babe—a personal craving to survive.

NEW MOON HAFTORAH

(ISAIAH 66:1-24)

I hate your new moons, your appointed holidays,
God says. A boy sings the memorized syllables,
Koh aumar! Adonai, hashawmayim keesee.

God hates your empty rituals and sacrifices.
He says it's like watching you cut a dog's throat.
Machey-eesh ohveyach hazeh aureyf keleb.

Inhabiting the shrill voice of the boy who chants
Uncomprehending the mighty sounds, God says:
Behold, the faithful city has become a whore,

By fire and by the sword will the Lord plead with
All flesh that sanctify themselves and hide in
Gardens to eat the meat of swine and of mice.

Gestures of worship disgust God. The boy sings
Faithfully the disintegrating words, *Losheh
Kay-awkh*, like one whom his mother comforteth.

He will make, between this new moon and the next—
The child's voice dares to promise in the old words—
Ahl-akhat, ehrkhat: new heavens and a new earth.

GENESIS

Where was the kiln, what was the clay?
What drove the wheel that turned the vessel?

Who started the engine so late at night?
Which was the highway across the hills?

Why did the animal turn on its keeper?
How did the preachers forge the bells?

I drank the shadows, I studied the shell.
I heard the rain and I took the wheel.

SAYINGS OF THE OLD

One of them said of mules: A creature willing
To labor for you patiently many years,
Just for the privilege to kick you once.

Few men are as good as their fathers, said another,
And most are worse, in the entropy of time,
Though some have said, My child—I am well traded!

One I know said to his son, So now we see you
On television: you're a celebrity now—
But then, you've been a celebrity all your life.

Something inside them, patient as a mule
That pulls the plow of being through the decades,
Has watched the stalks of fashion rise and fall.

"Celebrity" may have meant, "I think my wife
Always has treated you as better than me."
The Ibo say, An old man sitting down

Can see more things than a young man standing up.
But sooner or later, the mule kicks all alike:
The young, the old, the stalks of crops and weeds.

One hates the sanctimonious Buddha-goo
But loves to meditate. To think one word
And the breath balanced on its floor of muscle

Falling and rising like years. The brain-roof chatter
Settling among the eaves. All falling and rising
And falling again, a calm brute rhythm of hooves.

GRIEF

I don't think anybody ever is
Really divorced, said Lenny. Also,
I don't think anybody ever is
Really married, he said. Because

English was really his second language
And because of Yiddish and its displaced
Place in the world, he never really
Believed in his own prose. He wrote

Sentences the way a great boxer moves.
Near the end he told me, "I'm in Hell"—
Something Lenny might have said about
Hunting for a parking space in Berkeley.

Mike too was himself. His last month,
Too weak to paint or make prints,
He sat and made drawings of flowers:
Ink attentive to rhythms of beach rose,

Wisteria, lily—forms like acrobats
Or Cossack dancers. Mike had a vision
Of his body dead on his studio floor
Seen from high above—he didn't feel sad

Or afraid at seeing it, he said, just
Sorry for the person who would find it.
You can't say nobody ever really dies:
Of course they do: Lenny died. Mike died.

But the odd thing is, the person still makes
A shape distinct and present in the mind
As an object in the hand. The presence
In the absence: it isn't comfort—it's grief.

IN THE COMA

My friend was in a coma, so I dove
Deep into his brain to word him back. I tried

To sing *Hallelujah, I Just Love Her So* in
Ray Charles's voice. Of course the silence grew.

I couldn't sing the alphabet song. My voice
Couldn't say words I knew: *Because I Could
Not Stop For Death, He Kindly Stopped For Me.*

I couldn't remember the Dodgers and the Giants.

I tried to tell him the stories he and I
Studied when we were young. It was confused,
The Invisible Man was laughing at how a man
Felt History jump out of his thick fair head
And beat him half to death, as being the nightmare
Out of which Isaac Babel tried to awake.

The quiet. *Next time won't you sing with me.*
Those great diminished chords: *A girl I know.*

The cold of the coma, lightless. The ocean floor.

I struggled to tell things back from decades gone.
The mournful American soldier testifying
About My Lai: *I shot the older lady.*

Viola Liuzzo, Spiro Agnew, Jim Jones.

And by the time I count from one to four
I hear her knocking. Quiet of the deep,
Our mouths are open but we cannot sing.

THE CITY

I live in this little village of the present
But lately I forget my neighbors' names.
More and more I spend my days in the City:

The great metropolis where I can hope
To glimpse great spirits as they cross the street,
Souls durable as the cockroach and the lungfish.

When I was young, I lived in a different village.
We had parades: the circus, the nearby fort.
And Rabbi Gewirtz invented a game called "Baseball."

To reach first base you had to chant two lines
Of Hebrew verse correctly. Mistakes were outs.
One strike for every stammer or hesitation.

We boys were thankful for the Rabbi's grace,
His balancing the immensity of words
Written in letters of flame by God himself

With our mere baseball, the little things we knew . . .
Or do I remember wrong, did we boys think
(There were no girls) that baseball was the City

And that the language we were learning by rote—
A little attention to meaning, now and then—
Was small and local. The Major Leagues, the City.

One of the boys was killed a few years later,
Wearing a uniform, thousands of miles away.
He was a stupid boy: when I was captain

If somehow he managed to read his way to first,
I never let him attempt the next two lines
To stretch it for a double. So long ago.

Sometimes I think I've never seen the City,
That where I've been is just a shabby district
Where I persuade myself I'm at the center.

Or: atrocities, beheadings, mass executions,
Troops ordered to rape and humiliate—the news,
The Psalms, the epics—what if that's the City?

Gewirtz, he told us, means a dealer in spices.
Anise and marjoram used for embalming corpses,
For preserving or enhancing food and drink:

The stuff of civilization, like games and verses.
The other night, I dreamed about that boy,
The foolish one who died in the course of war:

He pulled his chair up so he faced the wall.
I wanted him to read from the prayer book.
He didn't answer—he wouldn't play the game.

THE WARMING

Young men like my uncles in olden times would "croon":
Walking or at work, a musical inward groan:

The blue of the night meets the gold of the day.
Ramona. Dance, Ballerina. Too-ra-loo-ra-lay.

I asked my mother, why did they sing like that?
Her enigmatic answer: *They're in heat.*

Stopped at a light just now a guy in his van
Their same age, sound system blasting, windows down.

We men like sounding hot. Or warm and charming—
Even folk singers who rhyme about global warming.

"All music's folk music," said the great musician,
"Horses don't sing." (But they do play percussion.)

Souls deepest in hell don't burn, they're wedged in ice.
"You're full of hot air." But hot breath can be nice.

Blood, color, class, religion co-author your drama:
A politician makes hay in Oklahoma

By saying he doubts Darwin and climate change.
A kayak to Nyack. Home, home on the range.

Elect you, sigh for you, die for you. Our systems fed
By long-dead life that rotted to our sweet crude—

Warmth, movement, light and all our musical racket.
Lipstick traces. How we do. An airplane ticket.

High volume, gasoline roar, an amplified voice
Keening its meaning—will we die of all this?

CUNNING AND GREED

An orchid that mimics an extinct female bee survives
Persisting for generations with untouched pollen
Stagnant inside it: an unmated simulation becoming
A funeral portrait. Floral, archaic as rhymed verses.

Near the end Uriah Heep says, *David Copperfield,*
I've always hated you, you've always been against me.
Copperfield retorts, *As I've told you before, it's you,*
Heep, who have been against the whole world. It's not

Exactly our fungicides killing the world's bees.
The theory is, rather, the fungicides make the bees
Die from our pesticides, otherwise harmless. Or,
Maybe it's the other way around, who knows?

Your artful greed and cunning—against the whole world.
And never yet has there been any greed and cunning
That did not do too much and overreach themselves,
It is as certain as death! So Copperfield tells his enemy—

The saying is, "An enemy is as good as a Buddha,"
Meaning, you ought to learn to attain tranquillity
From having someone against you. I get it, but it does
Make me feel skeptical, like Heep—tell it to the bees!

Artful Uriah. Orchid. Author. Doomed bees brewing
Honey. *As certain as death—Or*, says Heep, *as certain
As that school that taught me from 9 to 11, that labour
Was a blessing. From 11 to 1, that labour was a curse.*

DREAM MEDICINE

Aspiring, beset by failures, a Crow warrior
Longed for a vision to bequeath his children.
He fasted. He sang. He sliced some flesh from his finger
So Owl or Badger might eat it, and pay him back
With dream medicine for generations—as when,
Abed, becalmed, from nowhere we might think words
Of foregoers like Julius Marx: "What has posterity
Ever done for me?"—beguiling, acerbic.

Playing with a hatchet, I blundered a sliver of meat
Off my own fingertip, then gave false witness:
I blamed another boy for wielding the hatchet.
I was afraid of Truth itself. Months later
I tried to come clean, I told my father *I lied.*
He didn't seem impressed, in fact he seemed
Barely to listen. Maybe he knew already.
Or maybe Spider had eaten that piece of me

And spun a web to hex my father's hearing.
Or maybe it's just that he was watching TV.
Around the same time, from the Ford's back seat,

I asked him, did he believe in Life after Death?
His eyes in the rear-view mirror kind of shrugged,
"I don't know, probably not," he said. "Or maybe
Look at it this way: *you* are my life after death"—
Innocent yet adept. Bemused. Abrupt.

IMPROVISATION ON YIDDISH

I've got you in my pocket, Ich hob mir fer pacht.
It sees me and I cannot spell it.

Ich hob dich in bud, which means I see you as if
You were in the bathtub naked: I know you completely.

Kischkas: guts. Tongue of the guts, tongue
Of the heart naked, the guts of the tongue.

Bubbeh loschen. Tongue of my grandmother
I can't spell in these Greek characters I know.

I know "Hob dich in bud" which means I see you
And through you, tongue of irony. Intimate.

Tongue of the dear and the dead, tongue of death.
Tongue of laughing in the guts, naked and completely.

Bubbeh loschen, lost tongue of the lost, "Get away
From me" which means, come closer: Gei

Avek fun mir, Ich Hob dich in bud. I see you
Completely. Naked. I've got you in my pocket.

THE ROBOTS

When they choose to take material form they will resemble
Dragonflies, not machines. Their wings will shimmer.

Like the chorus of Greek drama they will speak
As many, but in the first-person singular.

Their colors in the sky will canopy the surface of the earth.
In varying unison and diapason they will dance the forgotten.

Their judgment in its pure accuracy will resemble grace and in
Their circuits the one form of action will be understanding.

Their exquisite sensors will comprehend our very dust,
And re-create the best and the worst of us, as though in art.

HORN

This is the golden trophy. The true addiction.
Steel springs, pearl facings, fibers and leathers, all
Mounted on the body tarnished from neck to bell.

The master, a Legend, a "righteous addict," pauses
While walking past a bar, to listen, says: Listen—
Listen what that cat in there is doing. Some figure,

Some hook, breathy honk, sharp nine or weird
Rhythm this one hack journeyman hornman had going.
Listen, says the Dante of bop, to what he's working.

Breath tempered in its chamber by hide pads
As desires and demands swarm through the deft axe
In the fixed attention of that one practitioner:

Professional calluses and habits from his righteous
Teachers, his dentist, optician. A crazed matriarch, hexed
Architect of his making. Polished and punished by use,

The horn: flawed and severe, it nestles in plush,
The hard case contoured to cradle the engraved
Hook-shape of Normandy brass, keys from seashells

In the Mekong, reed from Belize. Listen. Labor:
Flip all the altered scales in the woodshed. Persist,
You practiced addict, devotee, slave of Dante

Like Dante himself a slave, whose name they say
Is short for *Durante*, meaning *Persistent*—listen,
Bondsman of the tool—you honker, toker, toiler.

TAKES AND GIVES

I gave my name and they took some blood.
He gave some marrow, whatever it takes.
It took some time and it did some good.
We gave out the story, we took it for true.
Whatever was true, that was the story.

She gave up the ghost, she took her time.
Did she take his name, did she keep her own?—
Whichever it was, it was all the same.
Whatever was true, that was the story:
I gave my name and they took some blood.

CEREMONY

At the end of the story,
When the plague has arrived,
The performance can begin.

Displacing flimsy heaven
And its contraptions, now
Come practical urgencies:

Getting the price of salvation,
Divined from the guts of birds
Or from cruciform insects. Like

The savior Oedipus, kittens
Are histrionic: defiant swagger
Then ritual flight in terror.

"The soul of the cat is the form
Of its body." In Christendom,
Civic mourners were hired

To walk the stricken city ways
Chanting: "*I am sick, I must
Die—Lord have mercy on us.*"

EVOLUTION OF THE HOST

The primate that rose to dominate that planet
Communicated with its peers in a code of grunts
Exhaled from the orifice of ingestion and shaped
By lips and inner membranes, muscles and teeth.

The creature communicated with its descendants,
By memorizing chains of those same brute sounds
In patterns urgent as the dance of a worker bee
Miming the distance and bearings of the pollen.

In the tongue of mare's milk drinkers, *host* and *guest*
Are two pronunciations of one ancient word:
Khoust: meaning sacred obligations between
A stranger who accepts bread and one who gives it.

Or even older, the *khoust* was the massed foe:
The Philistine host, O Lord kill all their spawn.
The ghastly third, the ghostly other, who comes
Between my hunger and the sweet breast of the world.

GLORY

Glory is greater than success.
The one who threw the stone farthest,
The chorus chants in Pindar's incantation
Against envy and oblivion, was Nikeus,
Recalled now only in the poems of Pindar.
And when Nikeus grunting whirled the stone
Into the air, it flew past the marks of
All competitors and Nikeus's countrymen
Yelled his name, *Nikeus*, after the stone.
What is someone? the chorus chants
In Pindar's victory ode, *What is a nobody?*—
Both creatures of a day. At the Games,
Nikeus, his friends yelled, *Nikeus*,
And the syllables, say the lines Pindar
Composed for the chorus, echoed
From the cold mirror of the moon.

Tomatl, imported from Mexico, was once
Thought poisonous until a parson disproved
The misconception by eating one in church.

But that tale is itself misleading, a legend
Like truthful Washington and a cherry tree.
Cousin of Deadly Nightshade. Non-toxic. Exotic.

Columbus brought Italy the *pomo d'oro*
As Marco Polo brought the noodle from Asia.
In old American movies they sometimes say

"Tomato" meaning a woman, a word like "cupcake"—
Casual contempt we know to hiss at today.
My grandma called Italian people "noodles."

Spaghetti with red sauce is Aztec and Chinese.
Noodles from the East. Gold apples from the West.
Creole inventions time makes pure. *Tipico*

Italiano. So Nana could warn me in Yiddish
About Joe Cittadino, "Don't run with *luckshens*."
"*D'oro*" must mean those first imports were yellow,

And breeding made them red. Or maybe the name
Too is a misconception—the Sibyl knows,
Who wrote it aright on a leaf lost in the wind.

GENESIS ACCORDING TO THE SCULPTOR GEORGE SEGAL

The Spirit brooded on the water and made
The earth, and molded us out of earth. And then
The Spirit breathed Itself into our nostrils—

And rested. What was the Spirit waiting for?
An image of Its nature, a looking glass?—
Glass also made of dust, of sand and fire.

Ordinary, enigmatic, we people waiting
In the terminal. A survivor at a wire fence,
Also waiting. Behind him, a tangle of bodies

Made out of plaster, which plasterers call *mud*.
The apprentice hurries with a hod of mud.
Particulate sand for glass. Milled flour for bread.

What are we waiting for? The hour glass
That measures all our time in trickling dust
Is also of dust and will return to dust—

So an old poem says. Men in a bread line
Out in the dusty street are silent, waiting
At the apportioning-place of daily bread.

At an old-fashioned radio's wooden case
A man sits listening in a wooden chair.
A woman at a butcher block waits to cut.

What are we waiting for, in clouds of dust?
Or waiting for the past, particles of being
Settled and moist with life, then brittle again.

LIGHT

(After the Hebrew of Chaim Nachman Bialik)

Not rented not bought not stolen
Not borrowed, my light
Didn't come to me by luck
Or in a rich father's will:

Waiting its time, hidden,
Stubborn little light, as if
Hammered from living rock
I quarried out of myself—
Not much, maybe, but mine
Down to the bone.

When the rock shatters,
It flashes vanishing
Sparks for these verses
I make out of blood and air
And bits of marrow fire.

GÓNGORA: LIFE IS BRIEF

Bullets don't fly to the target any quicker,
A war-wagon's wheels muffled by the sand
Don't churn around a corner any quieter,
Than life quickly, quietly comes to its end.

Is anybody stupid enough to doubt it?—
Repeatedly, every day, the rising sun
Warns you: *Life passes, you're a falling comet.*
And every day it leaves the sky dark again.

Carthage gives witness only a fool ignores.
Don't waste yourself on shadows. Hours you abuse
Won't ever be forgiven—these easy hours,

This file of hours that scrape away the days,
These unforgivable days that open and close
One after another and swallow up the years.

RADIOMAN

He wasn't good at telling stories. He said
After we lost the outfit, meaning, they died.

He and the other survivor from their platoon
Wandered the battlefield till they lay down.

They slept. And when he woke, the other was gone,
So he walked that Battle of the Bulge alone;

Trying to use his compass, heading West,
He happened across a unit that had lost

Their radio and the radioman. They took
Him in, the SCR still strapped to his back:

The handset harnessed behind him, out of sight,
The antenna at his ear. *We slept, we ate.*

I had another outfit, somewhere to be.
They had a radioman, and that was me.

THE SAWS

The old saw *dead as a doornail* is still dead as a doornail:
Whatever a doornail might be or was, long lost in the dark,

The dark, the dark—not always deepest before dawn, Pal.
Back then, passing a graveyard you might actually whistle:

No walk in the park, a black back street back in the day.
Zombie sayings, Buddy, worn thin as a dime. Ghostly,

Generated by generations, they still stagger the castle,
Wan, rife. Benighted or bedazed by the March of Time,

Time, time. Sayings hardly ever anymore called "saws": *Kiss
The cat and you kiss the fleas*. And *That's the story of my life*.

ACKNOWLEDGMENTS

Grateful acknowledgment is made to the periodicals
in which some of these poems first appeared,
sometimes in different form: *AGNI*, *The American
Scholar*, *The Cortland Review*, *New Ohio Review*,
The New Yorker, *The New York Review of Books*,
The New York Times, *Ploughshares*, *Plume*,
Poetry, *Salmagundi*, *Threepenny Review*.